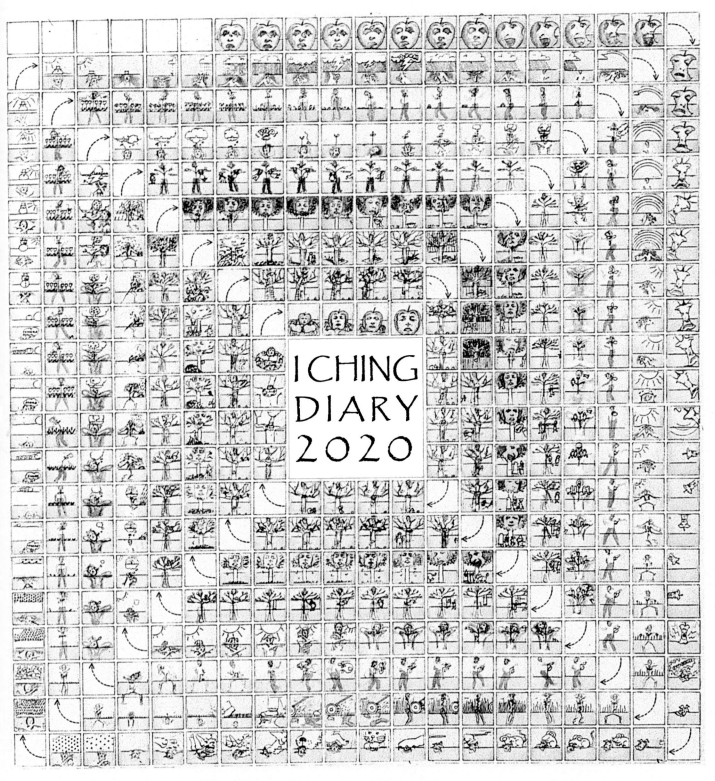

I CHING DIARY 2020

Growing through Change in the Age of Corona.

Kirk Chernansky

To order additional copies of this book, contact:
Xlibris
844-714-8691
www.Xlibris.com
Orders@Xlibris.com

ISBN: Softcover   978-1-6698-1599-0
        Hardcover   978-1-6698-1600-3
        EBook   978-1-6698-1631-7

Print information available on the last page

Rev. date: 03/28/2022

"To every thing there is a season, and a time for every purpose under heaven"

Ecclesiastes 3

INTRODUCTION

It is not uncommon that the antidote to something unpleasant exists within reach, if we only knew where to look. Jewelweed, after all, often grows near poison ivy and has the ability to neutralize its sting. For me, the *I Ching* has proved to be the antidote for the emotional toll of social distancing during the pandemic. Perhaps it is no coincidence that China, where the virus first took hold, is also the birthplace of this book of wisdom for coping with change.

The Art of Change

I began creating art based on *I Ching* hexagrams over twenty-five years ago using the image of an apple for inspiration. My family has a tradition of venturing every fall to a favorite apple orchard, and over the years, I had come to appreciate the apple as a symbol of regeneration and life. The little apple tree images seemed to work well with the hexagrams from Brian Browne Walker's *I Ching or Book of Changes: A Guide to Life's Turning Points* that I had begun to study at the time.

The writing of my blog was a response to events as they unfolded during 2020 using the *I Ching* as a guide for coping. The images of an apple tree's struggle to overcome the obstacles to growth served as an artistic device to underscore nature's way of adapting to change. For my first blog entry, I chose hexagram #47 "K'un," which is roughly translated as "oppression." It seemed fitting that as we entered into a state of confinement due to the pandemic, I begin with this hexagram using its Chinese Hani script depicting a tree that is confined.

The Process: Crisis and Opportunity, Two Sides of a Coin

Each week of 2020 seemed to present another crisis, which became an opportunity to consult with "the Sage." Though the practice of *I Ching* calls for the random throwing of coins to determine a hexagram reading, I decided to choose for myself the hexagram that best captured events during the pandemic as it was unfolding. Without going into detail, let me explain that a "hexagram" is like a fraction, only instead of numbers for the numerator and denominator, it uses symbols representing different aspects of nature (earth, wind, fire, lake, heaven, thunder, water, and mountain). My hexagram images mimic this pattern using a horizon line that divides earth from sky. To me, this combination represents the world of humanity (the earthly perspective) intersecting with the divine (the spiritual perspective).

Homage to Marcel Marceau

Though Marcel Marceau's mime mastery is well-documented, his extraordinary experiences and sacrifices during World War II created the foundation for what Marceau later referred to as his "silent language of the soul." He was just fifteen years old when Germany invaded Alsace, forcing the family to flee from their home in Strasbourg. Later, Marcel joined the French resistance and was responsible for rescuing countless young men by falsifying identity cards to save them from German labor camps and leading children to safety across the Alps to neutral Switzerland. When his father perished in Auschwitz, Marcel found refuge in his theater background entertaining troops. Elevating people's spirits became a lifelong passion.

My apple tree images originated as a storyboard that, like Marceau's pantomime, became a form of silent storytelling. I wanted my blog to mimic the profound sensitivity that seemed to merge humor with pathos and make you want to smile and cry at the same time. Today, as we move through the pandemic, multiple environmental crises, and political unrest, it seems fitting to draw upon images of Marcel Marceau as a model of transforming life's pain into an artistic expression that touches the soul and gives us hope.

March 14, 2020
Restraint

K'UN/OPPRESSION

Yesterday, the president of the United States declared the coronavirus pandemic a national emergency. And so I begin this blog with what should have been a day of celebration. Instead, the annual St. Patrick's Day feast has turned to famine with Governor Pritzker's order to close all bars and restaurants. "The time for persuasion and public appeals is over," he said. "This is not a joke. No one is immune to this."

The *I Ching* suggests that "none of us escapes such moments; they are simply a part of living." But this is no ordinary moment, and the consequences are grave. The question remains, Are people willing to abide by the mandate? Kudos to those who are preventing the spread of COVID by staying home and out of the hospital so that doctors and nurses can care for those ill with the virus.

Today's hexagram K'un advises us to practice acceptance and be gentle with ourselves. So with that in mind, I bid farewell to 2020's St. Patrick's Day parade and the greening of the Chicago River. And "until we meet again, may God hold you in the palm of his hand."

—Hexagram #12, based on Brian Browne Walker trans.

KEN/KEEPING STILL, MOUNTAIN

April Fools' Day 2020 is clearly no joke. Dr. Anthony Fauci warned Sunday that there could be 200,000 total deaths from COVID-19 before the crisis is over. The guidelines for social distancing, which should have ended today, have been extended through April 30. If only this was fake news.

When situations trigger "fight or flight," adrenaline can be helpful, but ongoing anxiety over time takes a toll on the body. Today's hexagram offers ways to quiet strong emotions.

It advises sitting comfortably erect with eyes closed and just observing the flow of your bodily emotions. The simple practice of watching them come, linger, and go—without acting on them—allows you to gradually release the tension and clear the mind.

Last but not least, if worry thoughts arise over things you cannot control, turn it over "to the Deity for resolution." Make April Fools' Day a prudent day like the hexagram says. Be still "like a mountain" and let the Sage do the work.

—Hexagram #12, based on Brian Browne Walker trans.

April 6, 2020
No Way! —Way.

P'I / STANDSTILL (STAGNATION)

If you read the headlines, it appears the world has descended into darkness and decay. Schools are having to partially shut down along with travel, entertainment, and restaurant venues, putting a multitude of folks out of work and careers on hold. Like a deer caught in the headlights, we become stunned by the pain and suffering brought on by the pandemic or overwhelmed by our own personal loss.

Still there is hope in the saying "pain is inevitable but suffering is a choice." Today's hexagram encourages us to accept the inevitable painful periods of life by turning within and recognizing that external progress is unlikely right now. Only then can we shift from suffering and focus instead on examining the thoughts and attitudes that inhibit our progress. In the stillness, we can begin the process of moving closer to our higher nature where healing resides. There is a knowingness that in the midst of pain, growth and resilience can occur.

—Hexagram #12, based on Brian Browne Walker trans.

SUNG/CONFLICT

A friend of mine brought me a couple of improvised face masks this week. They consisted of what looked like two folded napkins with a punched hole on each side through which rubber bands could be attached to hook around my ears. Such a simple solution that brought relief to my growing anxiety about how to manage sewing my own mask.

Calm in the midst of scarcity is hard to come by. Three weeks into the "stay at home" mandate, there is competition between states and the federal government over limited supplies of respirators and personal protective equipment, fears about the depletion of toilet paper on store shelves, and a stockpiling of hand sanitizer that is being resold at a profit.

Today's hexagram states that "ultimately all conflict is inner conflict," and the way to resolve the discord is to not be drawn into it. It says that by remaining detached, you can regain a sense of balance. If acceptance is still not within reach, the *I Ching* advises us to seek assistance from someone impartial to gain perspective until the Higher Power can provide the correct solution. Thank God for friends who keep me balanced with their caring actions.

—Hexagram #6, based on Brian Browne Walker trans.

SUN/DECREASE

After reports that COVID cases had quadrupled and deaths increased sixfold, the mayor closed one of my favored outlets—the Lakefront Trail. My first thought was, *They're taking away my happy place! It's not fair!*

The *I Ching* tells us that when faced with extraordinary change, it is normal to want to resist and hold on to our old lives. But fighting with reality can only make the situation worse. Today's hexagram advises standing back and being mindful of where your thoughts are leading you.

Each of us is experiencing pressure to adapt to a crisis we never thought possible in our lifetime. The *I Ching* says that acknowledging the longing for what used to be gives rise to feelings of compassion for ourselves and others. Reducing the resistance to events we can't alter allows us to move toward change together with increased resolve.

So last week, I turned my mind toward another happy place. I organized a Zoom birthday party for my sister. It was a delightful experience that would not have occurred were it not for my willingness to accept what is and stop focusing on the "if onlys."

—Hexagram #41, based on Brian Browne Walker trans.

April 22, 2020
Earth Day

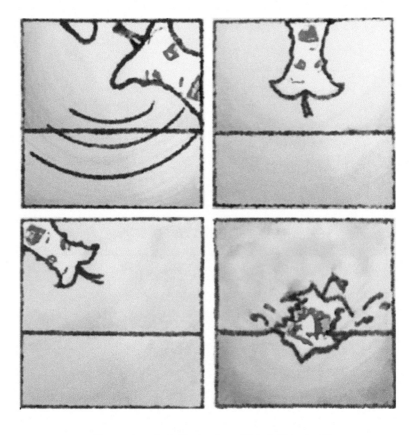

SUI/FOLLOWING

Today is the 50th anniversary of Earth Day. It was originally conceived as a day for people to take action on behalf of planet Earth. The celebration encouraged many to practice the four Rs: reduce, reuse, recycle, and repair.

It's hard to overcome the ease of just throwing things away in a culture built on consumption. But by doing so, we not only pollute our rivers and oceans, we deny ourselves a healthy feeling of regret or loss. The Japanese call this feeling "mottainai" and over time have created a culture based on a reverence for things that are old and worn. Instead of discarding things that are broken, they are lovingly repaired and preserved.

How do we as a nation do our part to repair the damage done to our Mother Earth? For those of us feeling powerless, the *I Ching* reminds us that acceptance of the current situation is not approval. It calls for actively seeking guidance and listening for truth, within and without, "even from unlikely sources." Perhaps then we can find "acceptance of the things we cannot change, the courage to change the things we can, and the wisdom to know the difference."

—Hexagram #17, based on Brian Browne Walker trans.

April 27, 2020
Rest, Reassess, Release, and Renew

KU / WORK ON WHAT HAS DECAYED

It is shockingly clear that care of the earth and human health are intertwined. This is especially evident in our black communities that overwhelmingly bear the brunt of the health and economic burdens brought on by the pandemic.

The *I Ching* states, "Receiving this hexagram is a sign that there is a defect in the attitude of oneself, another, or one's society that should be corrected." I begin to question my own actions. How might I be colluding with this system in which people of lighter skin lead healthier lives? If so, what can I do to change?

Today's hexagram recommends first making a sincere effort to understand the problem and then gently taking assertive action to correct any faulty thinking. This may require letting go of long-held beliefs or traditions that do not serve the greater good. Perhaps a change in perception can prevent further decay and renew the commitment to earthly and human wellness for all.

—Hexagram #18, based on Brian Browne Walker trans.

May 1, 2020
May Day! May Day!

MING I / DARKENING OF THE LIGHT

Today is May Day, a time to celebrate the beginning of spring with dancing and singing. "International Workers' Day" is also honored on the first of May, though it's hardly cause to celebrate this year. The jobless toll in America topped 26 million, with a hefty 4.4 million people filing for unemployment last week alone. That's highest since the Great Depression. Spring is feeling more like the dark of winter.

Today's hexagram tells us, "If we react to the lack of visible progress with despair and negativity, we extinguish our own inner light and block the aid of the Creative." The *I Ching* advises us to remember that much of the work of the Higher Power is hidden from us. We can assist "by remaining detached, accepting and reserved in the face of negative influences."

Though there's not much to dance and sing about, Congress did pass the $320 billion Paycheck Protection Bill last week. With current unemployment just the tip of the iceberg, progress may be slow, but the ice will melt in time.

—Hexagram #36, based on Brian Browne Walker trans.

HUAN/DISPERSION (DISSOLUTION)

So many people have shared support and appreciation for frontline health-care providers and essential workers through donations or nightly shout-outs for hospital staff returning from work. In the midst of the ongoing pandemic news, simple acts of kindness like my niece dropping off homemade cookies on our doorstep or friends posting messages of hope and videos of neighborhoods dancing and singing together at a distance are like a breath of fresh air.

The *I Ching* describes today's hexagram image as "that of a warm spring wind steadily dissolving winter ice." It tells us that a gentle, nonaggressive approach through prayer, meditation, or some form of sacred concentration helps us "overcome what is hard."

Imagery, music, and art are part of this as a means of releasing pent-up energy, and for me, working on this blog has done just that.

—Hexagram #59, based on Brian Browne Walker trans

May 10, 2020
Spring Fever

K'AN / THE ABYSMAL (WATER)

After a cleansing spring rain, my tulips have burst into full bloom. Gazing out the window, spring brings such a sense of renewal. It's easy to be lulled into a carefree state of mind. Forget the mask and the social distancing. Enjoy life!

But wait. The hexagram K'an reminds us of the troubling time and advises us not to yield to the desire for an effortless solution. Instead we are to flow through it like water while the Higher Power works out a solution.

This does not mean that we are not to act now but rather "not to act out of frustration, anxiety, despair or a desire to escape the situation." Remain open and let your inner "Sage" guide you step by step toward the lessons hidden within this pandemic.

—Hexagram #29, based on Brian Browne Walker trans.

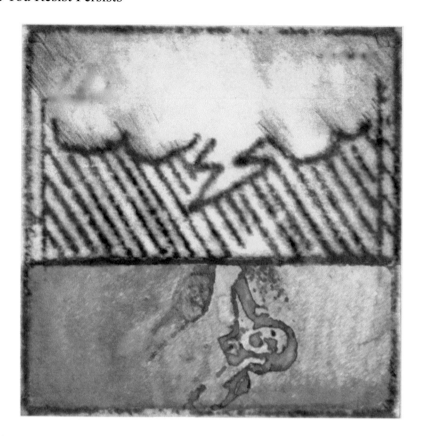

CHEN / THE AROUSING (SHOCK)

Sometimes when I think I'm not being listened to and what I'm saying is important to me, I'll repeat it louder and louder until I feel I've been heard. This irritates my husband no end and only escalates the frustration on both sides.

The incessant bombardment of COVID-19 updates has a similar effect. How often can I listen to the increased projections of the mortality rates, which is currently estimated to reach 3,000 deaths per day by June? Plus the seesawing perspectives of opening up versus hunkering down create further unsettling and escalating noise.

The hexagram "Chen" illustrates this pattern using the metaphor of thunder or "a continuing series of shocks" intended to bring about a correction in attitude. When feeling threatened by circumstances, the *I Ching* advises not reacting against the shocks that are there to teach and move us back onto the path of self-correction. Instead detach, withdraw into stillness, and realign with higher truth.

—Hexagram #51, based on Brian Browne Walker trans.

May 23, 2020
Gestating

CHUN / DIFFICULTY AT THE BEGINNING

We are entering the Memorial Day weekend known for its parades, picnics, and barbecues. This year, due to the pandemic, most events have been cancelled or significantly altered. Celebrating when so many are suffering loss triggers a sense of survivor's guilt. Donating resources and following guidelines are as much as I can do right now.

In response to my concerns about not doing enough, today's *I Ching* advises patience. It suggests, "No matter how fervently one desires to resolve a situation, to intervene impatiently now will only hinder the progress of good." The hexagram "Chun" uses the metaphor of "a blade of grass pushing against an obstacle as it sprouts out of the earth." It's a reminder that in nature, growth occurs at a steady, consistent pace and to act with tolerance and patience.

"Do not push aggressively, but do not give up." Let the light within be your guide.

—Hexagram #3, based on Brian Browne Walker trans.

May 30, 2020
"I Can't Breathe"

SHIH HO / BITING THROUGH

A new pandemic of racism seems to have spread quickly around the nation. To some, the symptoms seemed in remission, until the unrestrained actions of police brought an end to the life of George Floyd. His anguished plea, "I can't breathe," still reverberates in the mind and causes the heart to ache.

A friend's Facebook post described the headlines as sucking the air out of her lungs. COVID patients being placed on ventilators are also desperate to breathe. Is there some sort of existential connection between these events? Millions of years ago, fish dragged themselves from sea to land, driven by a need to escape predators. They were forced to evolve and learn to take in oxygen in a new way. Whether pandemic or systemic, it seems a large part of our population can no longer flourish in the world as it is. Desperation is highly motivating. Yet in times like these, the *I Ching* reminds us that "the administration of justice is the sole province of the Deity."

So what action can we take to rise above the chaos in order to respond effectively? Perhaps the answer lies in taking a deep breath and letting our inner Sage guide us in that first step toward higher ground.

—Hexagram #21, based on Brian Browne Walker trans.

KUAI/BREAKTHROUGH (RESOLUTENESS)

Last week, it seemed like the death of George Floyd had opened up a Pandora's box of pent-up anger. This morning, to relieve my growing agitation, I decided to read the responses of various leaders and participants on both sides of the protest, including all the living past presidents and recent contenders, a police officer, an activist, and a "good Christian woman." After reading their different perspectives, I felt uplifted. It was a reminder that when all the demons escaped from Pandora's box, the last to take flight was *elpis,* meaning "hope."

The desperate cry for justice in our country needs to be expressed, heard, and validated. But the *I Ching* reminds us that the seed of hope is nurtured with "tolerance and a spirit of calm equanimity." The people whose messages I read today shared that same insight in different ways. I am grateful to these role models who set examples that keep me from lapsing back into negativity. So as the *I Ching* advises, I "push forward," with increased awareness and resistance to the negative influences both within me and without.

—Hexagram #43, based on Brian Browne Walker trans.

CHIEH/LIMITATION

This week, I was confronted by someone I love dearly who expressed opinions that I found shockingly different from my own. Caught off guard and uncomfortable with my rising frustration, I took a deep breath to calm myself and suggested we just agree to disagree. Though the conversation was brought to an immediate halt, the need to be heard and understood was not.

Hexagram #60 addresses the need for boundaries but warns that when imposed rigidly, "can cause rebellion in the one on whom they are imposed." This became clear when I received an angry email the following day.

The *I Ching* advises us to "allow your interactions with others to take place within the limits of gentleness, tolerance and innocence." By first listening and understanding the other, we can create the opportunity for growth and reconciliation.

—Hexagram #60, based on Brian Browne Walker trans.

CHUNG FU / INNER TRUTH

After weeks of turmoil surrounding the death of George Floyd, the city is uniting in celebration of Juneteenth. One hundred and fifty-five years after Union soldiers informed African Americans in Galveston, Texas, of the end of the civil war and slavery, the struggle for freedom continues. Today's *Chicago Tribune* headline reads "A Day Like No Other," and indeed, the holiday brings a "welcome sense of positivity and encouragement."

Taking a brief respite from problems that seem overwhelming can be an effective coping mechanism. Taking appropriate action when possible is even better. The *I Ching* advises taking action by setting aside prejudices or hurt/angry feelings, then seeking to understand the other's point of view and what the "Sage is teaching us with the situation." When I take time to listen and look within for the truth, I can learn to lament injustice, repent my own unconscious collusion, and begin the process of reconciliation.

Truth be told, we all share a common need for love and acceptance. Each of us has the capacity to grow and heal by giving that precious gift to one another. Therein lies our freedom.

—Hexagram #61, based on Brian Browne Walker trans

June 27, 2020
The Cleansing Rain

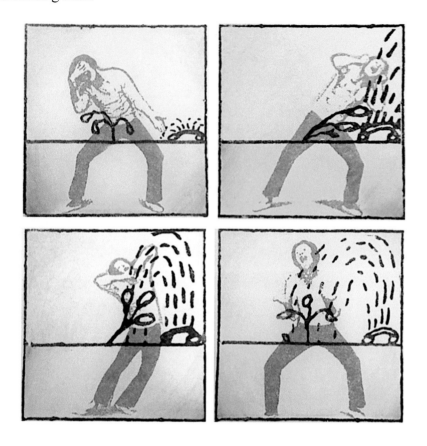

CHING / THE WELL

Our mayor opened up access to beautiful Lake Michigan this week, so we ventured out to the lakefront for the first time in over a month. The lake is not only a dependable source of pure water, it provides a deep well of spiritual nourishment.

Today's hexagram describes two wells of spiritual guidance—an external source of wisdom such as the *I Ching* and our own intuition that guides us within. Both must be developed and purified.

There is also a *Webster*'s definition of *well* that describes good health. What I choose to focus on and how I perceive it affects wellness. Like the wind that stirs up waves on Lake Michigan, there are times when I see only turbulence. The *I Ching* would describe this as drinking from the muddied well of negativity. It advises me to let go of the external focus on faults and instead look beneath the surface to the internal clear well within.

So today I feel refreshed as I focus on the lake and let go of worldly concerns. Only then can I find in the stillness within the guidance I need to respond effectively to life's stressors. With that in mind, I write today's blog and wish all who read it well.

—Hexagram #48, based on Brian Browne Walker trans.

CH'IEN / THE CREATIVE

Two hundred and forty-four years ago, a handful of patriots gathered together in a small room to confirm in writing their commitment to their vision of a new nation. It was a work of brilliance, creativity, and compromise. Its signing set in motion events that, over time, transformed governments around the world. The deep longing for liberty inspired the sacrifice needed to create change. That longing still exists today.

Celebration of the Fourth of July in the year of 2020 begs us to answer for ourselves the same question these men must have asked themselves. "What is it I visualize for my nation and its future?" If it is true that our thoughts, feelings, and beliefs have the power to create our reality, then let us clearly conceive, wholeheartedly desire, and sincerely believe in a nation that truly supports "life, liberty and justice for all."

Today's hexagram speaks to the power of creativity. When acted on with humility, patience, and receptivity to the truth, an "outpouring of benevolent energy from the heavens makes possible profound progress." Our forefathers created a nation based on their vision of the future. So now must we.

—Hexagram #1, based on Brian Browne Walker trans.

HSU/WAITING (NOURISHMENT)

I've always liked the idea of cocooning. It can very helpful, especially when ill or injured. Over the last few months, the coronavirus has resulted in an extended cocooning for many of us who are attempting to abide by the science-based directives of staying safe. There is a strong desire to rebel or ignore the recommendations and escape the cocoon.

Today's *I Ching* says, "There is a situation at hand that cannot be corrected by force or external effort." Could it be that the COVID-19 infections spiraling out of control in states that opened up early is an example of that? Today's hexagram reminds me that when I act on negative impulses, I interfere with what the higher power is working to accomplish.

There must be a butterfly in there somewhere if I can just wait long enough.

—Hexagram #5, based on Brian Browne Walker trans.

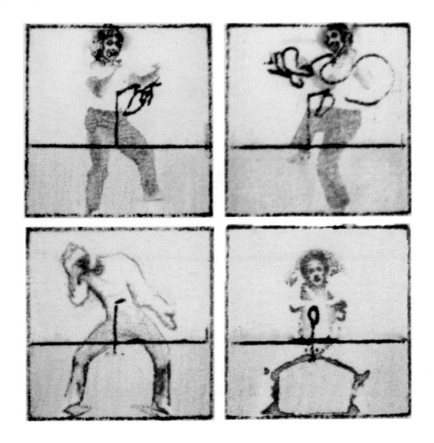

HENG/DURATION

A towering figure of Civil Rights died today. After a week of honoring his legacy, John Lewis will be going home to Atlanta, Georgia, to be laid to rest.

Resting is not a word John was comfortable with. Quite the contrary, he was a man of action—nonviolent action. His commitment and strength of conviction despite overwhelming setbacks and threats to body and spirit were an inspiration to many.

Much has changed in the sixty years since Lewis began his slow but steady march toward the cause of racial justice. Though he has been released from his earthly bonds, we remain to do the work that is unfinished. Today's hexagram captures the John's spirit of "encouragement to endure, to move ahead by abiding in what is true and correct" or, as John would say, "good trouble."

—Hexagram #32, based on Brian Browne Walker trans

July 19, 2020
E Pluribus Unum

PI / HOLDING TOGETHER (UNION)

What is herd immunity? Today's *Chicago Tribune* says that some argue precautions be lifted so enough people become sick in order to achieve it. It's a lousy idea and one that epidemiologists take issue with.

If indeed, we are all dependent upon one another to stay well, then how do we transcend the differing opinions that keep us ineffectively divided? Today's hexagram gives us three actions we can take: (1) "holding firm to one's own inner truth…striving always to remain balanced"; (2) remaining steadfast "against the effects of fear, doubt, despair"; and (3) remaining inclusive while joining with others of like mind to provide a sense of family for those in need.

At the suggestion of a friend last week, I listened online to the "2020 Race Amenity Day Conference" whose theme was "E Pluribus Unum." Perhaps it would be helpful to rise above the herd with this vision that they shared of community and oneness:

> *Ye are the fruits of one tree and the leaves of one branch.*
> *Deal ye one with another with utmost love and harmony*
> *with friendliness and fellowship. So powerful is the light*
> *of unity that it can illumine the whole earth.* (Bahá'u'lláh)

—Hexagram #8, based on Brian Browne Walker trans.

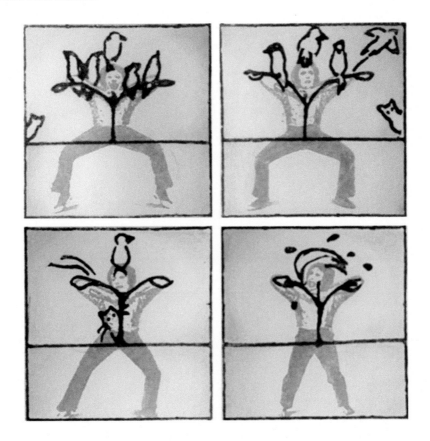

SHIH / THE ARMY

Last Sunday's *New York Times* magazine described a battle going on between public health and private liberty. It appears that the science behind ordering people to wear masks for the greater good is losing ground. With rising COVID cases and a second wave anticipated this fall, where or in whom do we place our trust?

Today's hexagram "Shih" uses the metaphor of a powerful army as a guide for evaluating an effective leader before entering into battle. It says that to maintain the allegiance of his soldiers, a general needs to show "superior conduct and even-handed treatment." One who uses force will likely be abandoned when most needed.

The *I Ching* says, "In times of war it is desirable to be led by a cautious and humane general." Sounds simple, but wait. It also reminds us that we can't just look outside ourselves for guidance. "Your chances of success will be determined by how you conduct yourself within and without." Honest and honorable actions can pave the way toward achieving the victory of peace of mind.

Some find that peace by wearing a mask; others in having freedom of choice. Only you can decide. Let your divine nature lead the way.

—Hexagram #7, based on Brian Browne Walker trans.

YU/ENTHUSIASM

Last week, I watched the film of the Broadway show *Hamilton* and was struck by its electrifying energy. Lin Manuel-Miranda's vision of a diverse, inclusive nation of leaders rapping the sounds of revolution and freedom helped make Broadway history and inspired a whole new generation to learn about the makings of a democracy. The *I Ching* tells us that success is achieved when fervor for what is right draws people together.

Today's hexagram "Yu" speaks about two kinds of enthusiasm. In the play, the character of Aaron Burr exhibits a kind of enthusiasm driven by the ego's need for recognition, power, and influence that ultimately leads to his downfall.

Hamilton, though not without flaws, possesses the kind of enthusiasm driven by his ideals. His eagerness to create a new form of government leads to his success as a prime mover in the course of history.

Though Hamilton died a tragic death, his passion lived on in his wife, who documented his story so that a play could be written about it two centuries later. So many doors were opened because of one man's proper enthusiasm.

—Hexagram #16, based on Brian Browne Walker trans.

August 8, 2000
Contemplating Possibilities

KUAN/CONTEMPLATION

Carl Sandburg said, "Nothing happens unless first a dream." In his poem "Chicago," he famously imagined us as a "a city of big shoulders…fierce as a dog with tongue lapping for action, cunning as a savage pitted against the wilderness." It seems his dream of our city became a nightmare last week, when both police and protesters were injured in a confrontation in Grant Park.

Meanwhile, Damon Williams has another dream of our city. As an organizer and member of the Black Abolitionist Network, he remains committed to creating within Chicago "a space grounded in love and community…a place to imagine and build healthier relationships between human beings."

According to today's hexagram, the Chinese word *kuan* can mean either "contemplation" or "setting an example." Like Williams, people around Chicago are doing both by detaching from conflict and taking time to contemplate a better outcome. The *I Ching* suggests that doing so with an attitude of acceptance and tolerance helps to clear a path to finding solutions aligned with higher principles that attract others to the cause.

So it was that on Friday in Freedom Square, folks came together to set up tents and offer food, clothes, and other services for free. Three miles away in Humboldt Park, police and residents worked together to tackle crime problems within the community. At an event on Harding, a marcher led his group in a prayer for police. Sandburg also wrote, "Come and show me another city with lifted head singing so proud to be alive and coarse and strong and cunning." It's a dream I can relate to.

—Hexagram #20, based on Brian Browne Walker trans.

August 15, 2020
Family

CHIA JEN / THE FAMILY (THE CLAN)

School is starting throughout most of the country in the next few weeks. Everywhere there is concern about how to provide education while protecting the health of our children, families, and teachers. The pressure is tremendous with conflicting expectations complicated by the digital divide, homework gap, and ZIP code inequities. Every option seems to have a downside. There is no one-size-fits-all approach. Yet it seems we look to government and schools to tell us what to do.

Ultimately, the welfare of each child resides in the hands of the parent. "The *I Ching* teaches that all clans must have a superior person at their center if they are to prosper and succeed." Today's hexagram reminds us to focus on our own development in order to generate the qualities of correctness necessary for improving our family, our workplace, our nation, and the world community.

Today I pray for parents who must make a decision concerning their child's education in the era of COVID. May each of them draw strength and guidance from an inner truth that emanates from the wisdom of their creator.

—Hexagram #37, based on Brian Browne Walker trans.

August 22, 2020
In the Midst of It All…

PI/GRACE

The word *grace* has different meanings in different cultures. The English dictionary describes it as having poise or charm. The Latin origins are rooted in the word *gratus*, related to being grateful. The biblical interpretation refers to the love and mercy given to us by God. All are aspects of an internal strength that the *I Ching* says is characterized by "steadfast devotion to the principles of humility, simplicity, equanimity and acceptance."

Where is the grace in the midst of a pandemic, the hostilities of a political race, or racial unrest? Look closely, it's all around you. It's in the tearing of an eye, the sound of a sigh, the touch of a gentle breeze. It rings loudly in church bells and softly in wind chimes. It cries out in the howls of a dog or gently in the purr of a cat. Yes, there's even grace in the shout of protesters and in the stillness when we kneel to pray for them.

Grace longs to be experienced. Know that its quiet strength can overcome all else.

—Hexagram #22, based on Brian Browne Walker trans.

August 29, 2020
There but for the Grace of God Go I

TING / THE CALDRON

The forest fires in California burn unrelentingly while Hurricane Laura pounds the shores of the Gulf Coast. I begin to think that chaos reigns, and I am lucky to be far away from it all. A sense of survivor's guilt quickly follows.

Today's hexagram "ting" consists of the symbols of wind and fire. Am I fueling the fire of agitation with my catastrophic ruminations? The *I Ching* tells me that the mind is a caldron, and whatever thoughts I put into it is my "offering to God." It advises me to turn my caldron upside down, pouring out the darkness so that it may fill again with light.

I turn my focus to images of the ancient sequoias that depend on fire for germination and new growth. There is order in chaos, though I cannot fully see or understand it.

Slowly my cauldron fills with a soothing sense of peace.

—Hexagram #50, based on Brian Browne Walker trans.

SUN / THE GENTLE

On August 18, our nation celebrated the centennial anniversary of the ratification of the 19th Amendment. It had taken women nearly 100 years of fighting for the right to vote before they finally were able to go to the polls on Election Day in 1920. Steady, persistent efforts of activists and reformers made that happen.

Today's hexagram speaks to the true meaning of strength. It is an image of a gentle wind dispersing storm clouds. "A wind that changes direction often, even a very powerful one, will disperse nothing—it only stirs up the sky. The wind that causes real change is one that blows consistently."

Susan B. Anthony and those who joined the movement suffered many abuses and a multitude of setbacks in their quest for equal voting rights. Their ability to maintain the momentum of a penetrating wind made possible their long-term success.

There is still much work to be done regarding questionable restrictions imposed on voting rights. What needs to happen? Do we have the will to change? Listen carefully, my friends. The answer is blowing in the wind.

—Hexagram #57, based on Brian Browne Walker trans.

September 11, 2020
In Memory of Nine Eleven

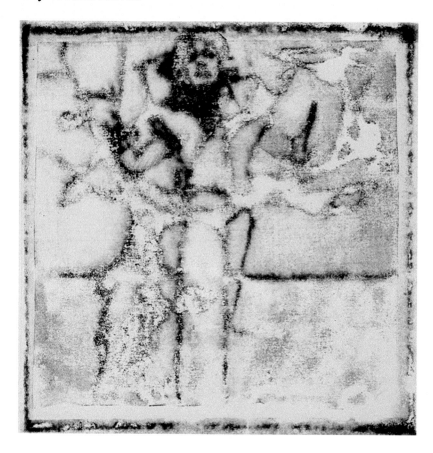

MING I / THE DARKENING OF THE LIGHT

There are no words to fully capture the horror that occurred on September 11, 2001. The hexagram "Ming I" describes a time surrounded by darkness and inferior energies. But there were positive forces at work as well. Through it all, police, firefighters, and volunteers at the scene responded with amazing courage and perseverance. They will never be forgotten.

Today's blog is dedicated to those first responders as well as to all those today fighting the wildfires that continue to burn out of control on the West Coast. We are so grateful for all the professionals and volunteers who offer help to others as they flee and seek shelter from both the flames and the pandemic.

—Hexagram #36, based on Brian Browne Walker trans.

September 18, 2020
RBG

TUN/RETREAT

Today marks the death of Ruth Bader Ginsburg. It seems appropriate that her passing falls on the beginning of the Jewish New Year representing a time both of rejoicing and of serious introspection.

When I reflect on Ginsburg's life and her influence not only on the Supreme Court but on my own life, I am deeply grateful. At the same time, I feel saddened at the thought of what it might be like now that we no longer have her quietly strong, steady presence during this dark time in our history.

Today's hexagram "Tun" speaks to the value of retreat in a time of darkness. Like the changing seasons, the *I Ching* describes a world in which forces of light and dark naturally ebb and flow, and we must adjust accordingly.

Ruth's Jewish faith was woven into her sense of justice and sustained her through many of life's darkest times. Regardless of our own religious affiliation, let us celebrate the completion of a life devoted to justice and equality so that we may begin the year anew with a commitment to upholding those values on which our nation was founded.

—Hexagram #33, based on Brian Browne Walker trans.

September 26, 2020
A Taste of Heaven

TA YU / POSSESSION IN GREAT MEASURE

Fall is apple-picking season, my favorite time of year. For the last 35 years, Mark and I have traveled to Indiana to gather bags of this tasty little fruit to share with neighbors and friends. It's a delight to wander the orchard with families, young and old, of many cultures—all seeking their favorite variety. There is no greed or lack in an open apple orchard in early autumn. The realities of the outside world dissipate, freeing up a new perspective of life.

It makes me wonder if perhaps the alienation and despair so many of us experience these days are a consequence of an inability worldwide to appreciate and share the abundant resources that the earth has to offer. The *I Ching* suggests that a change in perspective is all that is required. "By purifying thoughts, actions and attitudes long enough so that service of the true and good becomes your only goal in life, you come into complete harmony with the universe."

—Hexagram #14, based on Brian Browne Walker trans.

K'UN / THE RECEPTIVE

At no other time in my life has there ever been more radical change in a single year than there has been in 2020. Together, the social, political, environmental, and pandemic pandemonium have been mind-boggling. I prefer my change slow—like the change of seasons and the slow, steady, predictable rotation of the earth.

Today's hexagram K'un uses the image of the earth as an example of the benefits of yielding and accepting whatever changes come about. It suggests a time of quiet withdrawal and introspection to allow space for the "Creative to take root in our lives."

So I turn within, focusing on my inner axis that remains centered as the world spins around me. When my mind chatter subsides, I can begin to notice and accept those things I cannot change. In that peaceful state of mind, I can experience a change in perspective and return to "the path of independence and balance" again. Mindfully, I begin to observe life's soap opera (*As the World Turns*) without getting pulled into living it.

—Hexagram #2, based on Brian Browne Walker trans.

SUN/DECREASE

*To everything there is a season
and a time to every purpose under heaven.* (Ecclesiastes 3:1)

The trees are beginning to come alive with color. Soon they will be surrendering their leaves to the earth. All that beautiful foliage will be swept away to decay, but first it will dance its way to the ground with the ecstasy of a whirling dervish. What a glorious way to go! Nature is such a great teacher of how to move masterfully through change.

The *I Ching* is also a guide through life's turning points. Today's hexagram "Sun" describes how to manage a period of decrease. It advises us to accept and gently let go of our negative feelings, acknowledge our powerlessness over the current conditions of life, and return to the principles of our faith (or as the *I Ching* calls it, "the Sage").

Yes, there's "a time to be born and a time to die," but in the meantime, let us continue to celebrate life's beauty to the fullest.

—Hexagram #41, based on Brian Browne Walker trans.

October 17, 2020
20/20 Vision

CHUN / DIFFICULTY AT THE BEGINNING

Last week, Stockholm announced the 2020 Nobel laureates in physiology. The prize went to three Americans whose work contributed to the development of antiviral drugs for hepatitis C. The timing is of special significance since the coronavirus pandemic has revealed how important medical research is to societies and economies around the world.

Today's hexagram is one of optimism. It says that despite all the difficulties we face, if we can accept the pain and discomfort of chaos, the path to success will open up.

It's a lovely if not dubious vision, in the face of rising COVID infection rates and the political division. I guess that's what faith is all about. Trusting that when all seems lost, if we remain focused on our belief in ultimate goodness, we will be lifted across the divide.

So let us join in a leap of faith that in the year 2020, we'll be able to correct the cataracts of grievances and see clearly our true potential as human beings.

—Hexagram #3, based on Brian Browne Walker trans.

MENG / YOUTHFUL FOLLY

Lately, there have been a lot of conspiracy theories percolating around us. QAnon's claim that a cabal of satanic pedophiles is controlling the world sounds like the stuff of a Stephen King film. It makes for an absorbing distraction from painful reality.

Today's hexagram describes this escapist tendency as "folly: a characteristic of youth with little experience and of little wisdom." If indeed, we are more like children when it comes to dealing with the realities of life, then Halloween is a time to be playful with all those scary things that "go bump in the night." But let us be guided through the world of tricks and treats by a wiser, parental "sage" like an Obi-Wan Kenobi who can teach us how to overcome our fears of the unknown.

For both adults and children, this time offers an unusually horrific array of beasties. The *I Ching* encourages us to let go of our need to have answers and let the "Sage" lead the way through the host of goblins that lurk in our imagination.

May the force be with you.

—Hexagram #4, based on Brian Browne Walker trans.

October 31, 2020
Mischief

PO / SPLITTING APART

The election is just three days away. For many of us, it can't come soon enough. Though there's excitement about bringing an end to this tumultuous election year, there's also anxious anticipation about the possibility of postelection turbulence.

The hexagram "Po" describes this as "a natural state of affairs when inferior elements periodically come to the fore." Like Hurricane Zeta, there's no point in resisting what seems to be an inevitable conclusion to the tensions that have been building and undoubtedly exacerbated by the pandemic.

The *I Ching* encourages us to not let fear dominate but place our trust in "the Creative" to resolve the situation favorably. When we react to anger or fear impulsively, it fuels the divisiveness that splits us apart, not only from one another but from our spiritual path. We can respond to our emotions effectively and weather the storm by holding steady with patience and acceptance of both our own feelings and of those who feel differently.

—Hexagram #23, based on Brian Browne Walker trans.

November 7, 2020
Turning Point

FU/RETURN

It's an illusion I know, but the days seem so much darker since our clocks were set back last Sunday. As with daylight saving time, things change—sometimes abruptly, though other times incrementally. Today, we learned that Joe Biden is to become our president in January. Some see this change as a sudden onset of a darker period for the presidency, while others believe it's the long-anticipated fulfillment of brighter days ahead. Nonetheless, it's a turning point for all.

Today's hexagram "Fu" describes this turning point as "akin to the winter solstice." We cannot hasten the process of change. There is a healing at work in our country that will take time and effort.

The *I Ching* acts as a guide for times like these. It says to move gently through change like watching the rising or setting of the sun. It tells us to "let things develop naturally in their own way."

Whether it's spring forward or fall back, we should all make the most of this time by resting and gathering strength for the changes taking place.

—Hexagram #24, based on Brian Browne Walker trans.

November 14, 2020
Taking Flight

PI / HOLDING TOGETHER (UNION)

It's migration time! To celebrate the tens of thousands of majestic cranes that take respite from their long journey South, we planned to attend the annual Sandhill Crane Fall Migration gathering. The plans shifted abruptly when our friend called to cancel due to receiving a positive COVID test result.

The hexagram "Pi" describes this as a time for uniting in order to assist one another. But one of the heartbreaking aspects of COVID is that it discourages contact at a time when it is most needed. Fortunately, the *I Ching* has two requirements for holding together that do not require direct contact: (1) striving to hold fast to the One Power that is absolute good and everywhere present and (2) maintaining support to overcome "fear, doubt, despair and anger."

An ancient Japanese legend promises that the gods will grant a wish to anyone who folds a thousand *origami cranes*. My friend has developed a large circle of extended family over the years. May she take comfort in knowing that there are flocks of folks enfolding her in an origami flight of faith.

—Hexagram #8, based on Brian Browne Walker trans.

November 21, 2020
Giving Thanks

T'UNG JEN / FELLOWSHIP WITH OTHERS

At the height of the Civil War, Abraham Lincoln proclaimed a national Thanksgiving holiday for the final Thursday in November. In his proclamation, he entreated all Americans to ask God to "commend to his tender care all those who have become widows, orphans, mourners or sufferers in the lamentable civil strife" and to "heal the wounds of the nation."

This Thanksgiving may be as close to the original religious significance as Americans have seen since 1863. COVID has curtailed rituals centered on cooking and sharing a bountiful meal with family and friends. Politics has strained our relationships. Still, the need for coming together and sharing remains strong. How do we heal the physical and emotional wounds that separate us now?

Today's hexagram says that whenever we depart from "kindness, humility, correctness, equanimity and openness," we separate ourselves from one another and the spirit of love.

"An outward separation will come to an end in time. What is important now is to remain united in your heart with another. The path leads back to happiness."

—Hexagram #13, based on Brian Browne Walker trans.

K'UNG / THE RECEPTIVE

Did you know that there are two squirrel species in Chicago? What's more, they rarely live together. The gray squirrels reside in wealthier neighborhoods, and the rust-colored fox squirrels prefer less affluent areas. According to Professor Joel Brown who has been researching these four-footed Chicago residents since 1997, this is due to both environmental preference and temperament. Among other things, Brown discovered that because exurbs were more conducive to predators, the skittish gray squirrels preferred the relative safety of city life where dogs are leashed and cats indoors.

Chicago has also become known for its racial divide. Our residents of color have been separated into neighborhoods that suffer the most air, water, and chemical pollution, leaving them more vulnerable to disease.

Though our situation cannot be compared to squirrels and there are no simple answers, at the very least, perhaps we can reexamine our priorities and try to align them with the laws of nature and of God. The *I Ching* hexagram K'ung tells us to "bear with things as the earth bears with us: by yielding, by accepting, by nourishing…The solution to every situation is always available."

—Hexagram #2, based on Brian Browne Walker trans.

December 5, 2020
Healing the Sick

SUN/DECREASE

My father was a surgeon. He practiced according to the principles of the Hippocratic Oath, treating the sick to the best of his ability with warmth and sympathy. To him, it was not just a science. It was a calling.

Today there are multitude of doctors, nurses, and hospital staff caring for COVID patients at great sacrifice to themselves. Families of patients sacrifice as well, having to watch and grieve from a distance in isolation.

I believe that God works through all sorts of people. With more than 100,000 souls hospitalized due to the coronavirus, there is extraordinary need for everyone to do their part. Today's hexagram "sun" reassures us that if we do, things will get better. It tells us by "turning to the Higher Power for help, we emerge from the period of decrease stronger, healthier, and wiser." So take a deep breath, say a prayer, keep loving thoughts, check on a friend, wear a mask, and contribute whatever resources you can to take care of one another.

—Hexagram #41, based on Brian Browne Walker trans.

December 12, 2020
Waiting

FU/RETURN

This morning, I got up and made coffee. Craving that first cup, I was tempted to fill my mug before it finished perking. I resisted, knowing that what remained would taste like tea. Waiting can be hard.

This is the season of waiting—waiting for the vaccine, waiting for Santa, waiting for Congress to act on the COVID Relief Funds, waiting in lines six feet apart. The good news is we're reaching a turning point. Though hospitalizations have not yet peaked, the vaccination of hospital staff is in the works.

My friend sent me a link that showed me there are only 23 million people in front of me in line for the vaccine. And so I wait, knowing at least there is an end in sight. Today's hexagram says to let things develop naturally, allowing "time to rest and gather strength for a time of growth ahead." While the coffee perks, I plan the completion of my blog and let this season of goodwill and hibernation unfold accordingly.

—Hexagram #24, based on Brian Browne Walker trans.

LIN/APPROACH

After years of hanging lights on a freshly cut evergreen, we decided to finally make it easier on ourselves this year. Our new prelet artificial tree works just fine. There are so many uncomplicated ways to celebrate light during the holidays, whether it's the lighting of candles, searching the night sky for the "Solstice Star," or enjoying the warmth of an open fire (especially one that's gaslit).

This 2020 holiday has also kindled a growing light of hope as people become vaccinated against the coronavirus. After all, *corona* took its name from the obstruction of the sunlight when earth becomes enveloped in shadow during a solar eclipse. Goodness knows we've been passing through a very dark phase.

Today's hexagram "Lin" describes a movement toward light. It says that with tolerance and gentle patience, we will enter "a time of joy and prosperity." I trust that is playing out, and all our lives will be eased with the warmth of hugs again. The light of a loving embrace—what brighter light is there than that?

—Hexagram #19, based on Brian Browne Walker trans.

January 1, 2021
Begin Again

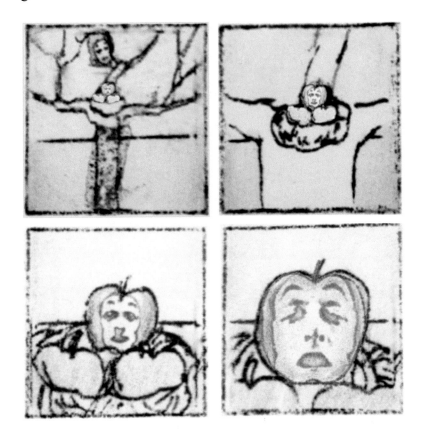

FU/RETURN

This is my final blog entry. A year ago, when I started journaling, little was known about the new virus that was spreading across the nation. So much has happened since then. It seems fitting that this New Year's Day as the first vaccinations are being given, I share with you the hexagram Fu, "a sign that we have reached a turning point."

Like jewelweed that grows near poison ivy and has the ability to neutralize its sting, the *I Ching* has been for me the antidote for the emotional toll of social distancing. Perhaps it is no coincidence that China, where the virus first took hold, is also the birthplace of this book of wisdom for coping with change.

It is true that there are still many profound obstacles our nation faces, but as the *I Ching* tells us, "One cannot force the completion of the change." And so we begin again "moving gently and innocently" into the next year while trusting that "the greatest adversity is past and the light is beginning to return."

—Hexagram #24, based on Brian Browne Walker trans.

EPILOGUE

November 27, 2021
The More Things Change…

When I wrote my final blog on January 1, 2021, and said good riddance to 2020, it seemed like a new beginning. Indeed it was—vaccinations had become increasingly available, and by June, daily deaths had dropped to under 400. There was a sense of optimism that with the onset of summer, things could return to normal.

Then things changed, or should I say didn't change. Though the vaccines were free to all American adults and teens, many declined to take advantage of them, and hospitals began to overflow again, primarily with the unvaccinated. Fueled by the Delta variant, the nation by October of this year had reached a threshold of 700,000 coronavirus deaths, with 350,000 just this year.

Nonetheless, by Thanksgiving, we were ready to resume the normality of gathering with our families and friends, only to find out the next day that there's a potentially more dangerous "Omicron" variant emerging in South Africa prompting new fears followed by a sharp decline in the stock market. So how did we get here? What advice would the *I Ching* give about this continuing conundrum?

According to Brian Browne Walker, "The *I Ching* takes a decidedly realistic view of the world. It doesn't mislead us into thinking that evil—in ourselves, in others, in the world at large—can be eliminated once and for all. It acknowledges that we all have in our characters both positive and negative elements and it teaches us to be led by our superior qualities so that our thoughts and actions can be free of inferior influences." Putting into practice the "principles of humility, simplicity, equanimity and acceptance" creates an inner strength that leads to success.

This is especially needed during life's turning points. Goodness knows the radically changing events of 2020 and 2021 have tested our ability to adapt and be successful. I hope these readings have provided some sense of balance and perspective in the midst of it all.

The *I Ching* is a book of ancient wisdom—an external source of guidance. Wisdom also comes from within. The text calls this inner source "the Sage." Others may prefer the name of "God," "Allah," "Higher Self," etc. Whatever your source, within or without, may you continue to find comfort and guidance in the presence of your Divinity as you move forward through the many unexpected twists and turns of life.

Based on Brian Browne Walker translation

Printed in the United States
by Baker & Taylor Publisher Services